Mad Woman

Emma F. Payne

Other Books by Emma F Payne

Thursdays with You

To those afraid to share their truth,

I believe you. You deserve the love you give others.

And to the other girls who fell victim to the same
monster as me,

You are not alone, and you are not crazy.

Warning

This content addresses sensitive subjects such as domestic violence and religious trauma.

Reader discretion is advised. If you or someone you know is struggling with these issues, please reach out to a trusted friend, family member, or mental health professional for support.

Introduction

I wrote *Mad Woman* during a profoundly challenging time in my life, as I was healing from an abusive relationship. The process of recounting my experiences in court was overwhelming, so I turned to writing as a means of coping. I completed the first draft in 2021, but at that time, I felt it was not the right moment to publish. Instead, I focused on releasing my first book, *Thursdays with You.*

Now, after continuing my journey of healing and finding the courage to speak out, I am ready to share my story. I hope that by doing so, others might also find the strength to share their truths. In *Mad Woman,* I speak with honesty and bravery despite the fear. This is my story, and it is my truth.

Mad Woman

Emma F. Payne

Mad Woman

Mad

You declared me mad,
And I withdrew to a madhouse
In hopes of escaping your presence.
Yet, upon my release,
I found myself once more in your company.

Now, after receiving 105 messages,
I remain resolute in my wish for solitude.

Emma F. Payne

Timing Is A Weird Thing

In the dead of night, sleep escapes me.
A relentless besiege in my mind.
Replaying, incessant,
The judge's cruel resolution —
To bare my soul, only to salt my wounds.

"Why the delay?" His accusation rings.
"Why endure in silence?" He interrogates.

Confused

They say women are confusing.
My *"no"* meant a *"yes"* to you.
My silence always did, too.
I was the one left feeling confused.

Emma F. Payne

Belonging

You arrogantly parted my legs as though
Entitled by some divine right —
Yet, they were never yours to claim.
They belong to me alone.

I Would Know

Through taste, by scent —
I would know him.
A tinge of bitterness and angst,
Sulfer.
An acidic pulse in my heart.

Something Kind

To be afraid and alone.
In a room with my mind.
I converse with a wall,
Waiting for it to utter back.
"Tell me something sweet," I beg.
Share with me something kind.

Inflammable

You soaked me in gasoline,
With a match poised by my side—
Ignited by your hands,
Eager flames danced in my eyes.

Emma F. Payne

Confess

I must confess my sins to you.
I drank the poison and forgave the snake for feeding it to
me.
I blamed myself for the scars from his bite.
I fed him my sins, and he spit them back in my face.
I confess.

Please, forgive me.

Too Young

I was always too young,
But that is precisely what you loved about me.

Emma F. Payne

Ignorance

Copper tang upon my tongue,
In a gown of malted hue.
I grieve the sweet, naive days,
My stolen ignorance from you.

Reflection

I covered all of my mirrors
So that I would not see myself.
A meer accident would have sealed Death
With a kiss.

Purgatory

You toyed with my emotions —
Manipulated my thoughts.
You conveyed a sense of inadequacy within me.

In a just world, you would reside in purgatory
For the rest of your days.

Haunted

With every night that passes
The memories of you fade,
But the memory of that one night,
Haunts me in my woken daze.

Unloved

When she fell, completely broken;
When her heart stopped.
That is when he decided to show love to her.

Heartless

It is cathartic to see all I can be
When I am "heartless."

Emma F. Payne

Isolation

In the period of self-evaluation—
The time of solitude—
I hope you found something within yourself
That you can truly love.

Plead

My words pain to be spoken;
To escape their prison.
Much like the way you pleaded
To be let inside;
Your desperation pressing
Against the walls I built.

Emma F. Payne

A Lovely Sin

I was always distant when I was with you.
Never once did you ask me where I was.
If you had asked, I would have lied.
I was not with you, but in her arms —
Safe and warm.

Oh, what a lovely sin.

Marigolds

I purchased some flowers to teach myself that
Loving was not only an option but a necessity.
When they wilted, I grew fonder of the beauty.
They emitted a veil of burning orange pigment.
More beautiful than anything
Our relationship was able to offer.

The Elephant

The elephant in the room was the energy radiating
From your existence.
It was our relationship.
The way you stared at me when I was crying out
For help through my motions.

Heavy

Your secret sealed within my mind —
A boulder sat in me.
A spread of lies to shallow foes —
Filled my life with cruelty.

Stalker

You pursued me across state lines,
As though no boundary could sever the chains you
forged.
Each mile stretched before me as an endless expanse of
dread,
For your presence clung to me like a specter,
Unyielding and insidious,
Draining my peace and tightening the noose of fear.
In every new place I sought refuge,
You followed with a merciless determination.
Your pursuit is a constant torment,
Rendering distance a mere illusion
Against the terror of your unrelenting chase.

Silence

My silence was a universe of dead ends.
A winding path that ever twisted and turned,
Forever leading nowhere.

Emma F. Payne

Trash

He is discarded, a remnant of refuse,
And his followers, mere flies,
They swarm around him —
In a haze of mindless thought.

A Phoenix

In the quiet morn of self-reclamation,
I stand, unburdened by yesterday's pressures.
No longer shackled by the remnants of your actions,
I seize the light that once seemed distant.
For I have faced grace, and I will rise
From the ashes of a past now powerless.
No longer do I bear the shame but rise as the phoenix
From the ashes of you.

Emma F. Payne

Everything I Was

I lost all sense of myself —
A quiet unraveling,
Where identity faded.

A gradual disintegration,
Where my edges blurred
Into the void of absence.

Falsified

You offered brief apologies,
A fleeting gesture
When your ego stung.
A momentary discomfort
For your bruised pride.

Emma F. Payne

Mauled

I'd rather be mauled by a bear
Than endure the quiet cruelty
Of being in the same room as you.
The bear's raw force is a welcome escape
From your cold presence,
Which cuts more profound than any claw.

You Thought

I wanted to own my form as you once thought you did,
To feel the strength and grace you once thought you
knew.

Emma F. Payne

They Take From Me

I am running out,
Slowly draining the well of myself
That I once poured so freely.
I give and give.
My hands open,
Only to find them empty,
While they take and take.
Drawing from me
Until there is nothing left.
Each gesture of generosity
It leaves me a little more hollow,
Until I stand here;
A vessel drained dry,
Seeking solace in what I used to be.

Stained

Your name bears the stain
Of deeds unkind.

Emma F. Payne

I Am

I am whatever I declare myself to be,
A reflection of my choosing.
I shape my identity,
But I am not bound
By the images others impose,
Nor by the people they see in me.

Bound

I was paralyzed. —
The fear I inflicted upon myself.
Each breath I took was tinged with anxiety.
A single anchor pulled me deeper still.
No rope bound tighter, none as cruel.

Emma F. Payne

I Did Nothing

I did nothing to deserve this,
Yet the heaviness of the world fell upon me.
I did nothing to invite this pain,
Yet, here I stand, bleeding out
For others to feel seen.

The Truth I Carry

You did everything
Within your power
To silence me,
To stifle my voice,
And make me fear
The truth I carry.

Emma F. Payne

Rape

It took me 26,280 days
To admit it was rape.
26,279 of those days
I was trapped.

> I am now free.
> Free to embrace both
> Reality and recovery.

A Minor

You told me to kneel
As you preached your gospel of lies.
I was told to worship your word with no consent.

Sacrifice

I did not say *"no,"*
Nor did I push you away.
I did not scream,
Nor did I flee.
I let my tears fall
As I laid paralyzed in fear.
I did not say *"yes,"*
But that silence was enough
For you to seize what you desired.
In your eyes,
I was a sacrifice,
Offered up to fulfill your will.

Sinner

You were the one who sinned.
Devoured my body
As if you had been starving for over a decade.

Emma F. Payne

Warmth

I felt a warmth rise within me,
But even as I tried to loosen my hair,
I could not help but make you plead
For me to surrender my body.

Baptism

You wanted a baptism,
So you drowned me in holy water.

Emma F. Payne

I Know Too Well

I have a killer in my mind,
A figure of a darker kind.
It hides in plain sight,
A haunting presence that I know too well.

Tricky

You tricked them all into believing I was the crazy one.
Used your charisma to charm them into lies,
Then prayed on Sunday for forgiveness for your evil
behaviors.

Emma F. Payne

Fault

Time and again,
I retraced the events in my thoughts,
Perpetually questioning,
"What fault lay within me?"
I bore the weight of blame,
For everything you did,
Believing it to be my failing,
That I had given a misimpression.

Yet, I see now that there was no self.
I was just a piece of flesh in your eyes.

Incapable

There were moments when
My memory faltered,
As if I was drugged and dragged
Until the very notion of up or down
Was rendered moot.
Yet, you seemed incapable
Of discerning *"yes"* from *"no,"*
So perhaps, in the end,
It mattered little.

Emma F. Payne

War

I went through life with bruises and cuts
From the battle we fought.

Wrong

I needed to bring you suffering,
Yet the victim endures
Far more than the perpetrator.
The victims walk into
A prison of their trauma;
A persistent Hell for being in the "wrong place,"
At the "wrong time," wearing the "wrong thing."

I'm Sorry

Even though he was the reason for her tears,
She did the only thing she knew.
She held him as he cried out his pathetic *"I'm sorry."*
While her clothes were still in tatters at the hands of a
monster

You Fucked Up

You do not even know who you are.
A rapist. —
To you
I was your girlfriend.
Obligated to give up
My body to you on a silver platter.
I no longer take pity on you
And your fucked up mind.

Emma F. Payne

Deception

The rumors spread —
A wildfire of deception.
They dance on the lips of those
Who know nothing.

Freeze and Fawn

I lay frozen with fear,
A barricaded door in front of me.
No salvation could reach me.
I stared like a deer in headlights,
Stunned by the darkness that had been thrust upon me.

Emma F. Payne

The First Time

It was supposed to hurt, right?
The first time.
I had always heard that,
But they never told me that it would scar me for life.

Victim Blaming

For the longest time,
I bore the weight of blame alone.
A victim of my castigation.

Emma F. Payne

Helpless

You held me captive as you desired,
In helpless proximity,
By your side, I lingered.
Little did you anticipate my departure.

Sacrifice

You told me that you would
Kill yourself —
          Or me,
If I was ever to give myself a voice.

Emma F. Payne

Free

I spent my days seeing
You everywhere.
Now, with humble pride confessed,
I no longer do.

Way To Heaven

I was not placed
Upon this earth to love you,
And loving you
Shall never lead to heaven's gate.

Emma F. Payne

Rare

You are a rare breed.
Damn, I wish I could say that
With truth in my voice.

I Mourn

I mourn the path that led me here. —
I grieve not only for the chances
That slipped through my fingers,
But also for the lost days of childhood.

Merciful

May God have mercy on you because I won't.

Punch

I hope the girls you punch
Punch you back.
I hope they say what they need to
To remove themselves from your grip.
I hope you are left with nothing of them.

Emma F. Payne

A Life In Me

My body ached in his presence.
In distance I am free.
Allowed to live a life in me.

Not Enough

I was nowhere near enough for you.
Not worth a measly glance.
Nothing left but an empty shell of myself.

Emma F. Payne

Monster

He shred every inch of my skin
With his cold, stale fingers.
Carving a path across my collarbones
And disappearing around my hips.
Tears puddled into my shoulders,
And ran down my arm in a thin trail
Like blood from my open wounds.

Sobering

Now that I am sober,
I can feel everything.

Emma F. Payne

Wasted Youth

My first kiss was poison on my tongue.
Tar thick with jealousy.
I was naive to think anything but.

No Escape

They say that you can escape into your dreams, but
Those are haunted, too.

Absconded by you.

Emma F. Payne

To Write Again

Thank you for the precipice —
For the abyss, where I descend —
To write once more, with an anguished pen.

Trigger-Happy

As you placed the gun in my trembling hand,
The very weapon you once threatened to use,
You pulled the trigger with a cold finality,
And with that act, you pushed me to the brink.

That's the last time you bring a gun to a knife fight.

Emma F. Payne

Cast Away

You cast me away,
Ensuring silence reigned —
Atop the desolate structure's crown.
Where nothing resonated.

Naive

No knowledge or warning
Of cold, dead eyes.
Young and naive to the signs.
A freight train ran into me.

Emma F. Payne

Trauma

Trauma is silent as it
Pounds, aimlessly, against my skull.

Moth To A Flame

A single moth to a flame,
Established in the loss of self.
Swallowed —
In a dimly lit room.

Ending

For once, I want to see
How the story in front of me
Ends.

Kneel

"Why are you not praying on your knees for me?" He implored.
Who needs to be on their knees praying for forgiveness now?

Emma F. Payne

Bare

You made me feel naked and exposed,
Even when I was fully clothed and alone.
Your gaze undressed me and
Stripped me of my defenses.

Devil In Disguise

You wanted to be my savior,
But you were the devil in disguise.

Stale

His breath was stale, and so was his personality.
Conversations with him felt like trudging through murky
waters.
Even his smile seemed practiced —
A brittle curve that never quite reached his eyes.

Ego

I will sit back and watch
As your ego is starved.

Emma F. Payne

The Universe

You may see me as small,
But I refuse to be diminished.
I have the universe inside of me;
A heart made of stars,
And a mind full of galaxies.

Love Without A Home

Love without a home is not love at all,
For the heart needs walls.
Love finds its dwelling, sweet as a poem.
Not in the vastness of endless skies,
Nor in fleeting winds.
Let trust be the mortar that binds the heart.
For love without a home is nothing but doomed.

Emma F. Payne

Boundless

Within me reside poems
Too profound for mere paper
To contain.
Needing a boundless medium.

Heartbroken

Every day, I woke up with my heart
Already breaking.
Aching for some form of safety,
That I was unable to secure.
The day had not even begun.

Saddened

In every portrait taken,
My gaze drifted, unanchored.
I stood with a smile,
Yet my eyes remained empty and distant.

Caged

Demons tormented me, imprisoned
Within a cage, I forged with my hands.
Their desires reverberated in the iron bars —
Torture of my design.

Emma F. Payne

Willing

The sea speaks honestly to those who dare to drown,
Its voice clear and unmasked beneath the waves' hold.

My Dance With Death

My arms were open.
Wide for death to dip me.
Swoon his way into my heart.
I faced Death's daring stare.

Emma F. Payne

Feast

Three days without an appetite,
Yet I am brimming with fullness,
Not from sustenance,
But from an unseen feast within my soul.

Not Your Normal Twenties

Not the usual cadence of youth,
Nor the rhythm of ordinary years —
These are not the twenties or teenage moments,
But a world apart, shifting and strange.

Just Maybe

Maybe those lies do not lace her lips like they used to.
Those swords may not scrape her back like you want
them to.
Maybe she has chosen to let go of every lie she was
Holding onto and surrendering herself to the earth.
Maybe she said *"no"* at just the right time.
Maybe she saved her heart while she still could.

Broken

Is it a wonder I broke—
When the weight of days
Pressed so heavily?
The heart, though steadfast,
Is but fragile clay,
Surrendering to the strain
Of never-ending burdens.
In the stillness of ruin,
Is it strange that pieces
Scattered wide and far,
When the pressures of existence
Demanded more than I could bear?

Emma F. Payne

Love Was Not One

Out of all the things you taught me,
Love was not one.

Immature

When I think of you,
I go back to high school.
I am not sure if you ever left.

Loss

The crumbling of my whole existence seemed inevitable.
The devastating loss of myself.

The Best Decision

The day everything changed
Was the day I chose to stop giving into your grip.
The day everything changed,
I chose myself over you.

Malnourished

Death clung to me more tightly
Than the ragged clothes upon my frail, malnourished
frame,
An inescapable shroud draped closer than fabric.
A presence more intimate.
Lingering in the hollows of my hunger,
Settling in the marrow of my weariness,
An eternal companion, more unstoppable than want.

Weary

An ill drum of a faint heartbeat—
A rhythm weak and wavering,
Soft against the silence.
In the stillness,
Its pulse falters,
A distant whimper of life
Barely touching the air.
This fragile cadence,
So easily lost,
Tells a tale of weariness,
A heart's quiet struggle
To maintain its beat.

Emma F. Payne

If I Burn

If I burn, you burn with me—
The fire, unstoppable,
Turning us into ash
Beneath my feet.

River's Edge

Heavy feet, like cinder blocks,
Rest at the river's edge.
Burdened and final,
Poised to plunge into the depths below.
They stand a solid stone.

Emma F. Payne

Mute

I feel mute from holding your secrets—
Words are caught in the stillness,
Timid, reluctant to emerge.

Grace

In this lightness, I seek grace,
A freedom from the load I bear,
Where each foot can rest easy,
Supporting the fragile self with ease.

Emma F. Payne

Relief

What can I say to stop the pain?
To still the throb
That resides in my chest?
Words seem frail, inadequate,
Unable to soothe the rawness
Or stem the tide of sorrow.
In the quiet spaces,
What relief can be found,
Or balm to ease this endless hurt?

Stone

To you, my heart is stone —
An unforgiving granite
Encased in an indestructible casing.

Emma F. Payne

The Mental Torture

In the darkened recesses of the mind,
There is ceaseless torment.
Each thought a piercing edge
Against self.
Time stretches, a heavyweight,
As silence screams within the soul.

Winning

If I say nothing, it never happened.
If I say something, I'm playing the victim.
There is no winning to you.
But I am playing your game,
And you're not winning it —
Each move a careful step
In the dance of strategy.

Emma F. Payne

Resurrect

Some stay behind bars only to resurrect
When the dues are met.

Projection

The feeling of inadequacy you bestowed upon me
Was almost the death of me.

Nothing

The voices in my head
Told me that I was undeserving of love.
I was diminished to nothing.

Nothing but "yours."

Threats

If I did not say *"I love you"*
With immense sincerity on my tongue,
You would take your life along with mine.

Emma F. Payne

Beneath the Waves

You will drown beneath your waves.
In its grip, the depths will claim —
The force of tides, your soul's name.
No refuge was found in the shifting sea.

Reacting

Am I overreacting?
Or am I just finally reacting to everything you put me through?

Emma F. Payne

Who You Are

Everyone sees you as someone else—
Even you have come to believe it.
You have worn the mask for so long,
It is hard to remember who you truly are.

Hate Crime

Because I fell for a woman,
Instead of at your feet,
You raped me back into the closet.

Emma F. Payne

04/07/2020

The joke is on you,
Hiding from the truth you cannot face.
I stood at the podium,
Bearing the burden of your shame and guilt,
Revealing the scars of your actions.
The judge recognized the truth and fought for me,
Yet I chose, again, to remain silent.

Remember

This is your reminder that I could say worse,
God as my witness.

Emma F. Payne

Do It Terrified

Wavering still, I spoke in fear.
Overtaken by trauma,
Screaming into the void.
I did it terrified.

Thank you so much for reading. Please feel free to leave a review on Amazon or Goodreads. Every review helps others find my work.

Hotlines

National Domestic Violence Hotline: 1 (800) 799-7233 or text "START" to 88788
National Suicide Prevention Hotline: call or text "HELP" to 988
National Sexual Assault Hotline: 1 (800) 656- 4673
The Trevor Project: 866-488-7386 or text "START" to 678678

About The Book

Mad Woman is a vulnerable collection of poetry that powerfully captures the journey of surviving abuse and the subsequent healing. Each poem reflects the complex emotions of trauma—pain, anger, and despair—while celebrating resilience and self-discovery. Through evocative language and vivid imagery, the poet challenges societal stigmas surrounding mental health and offers a safe space for readers to confront their own experiences. This collection is a testament to personal survival and a beacon of hope, inviting others to embrace their stories and find strength in vulnerability.

About The Author

Emma F. Payne is a passionate poet who lives in Owensboro, KY, with her wife and two beloved cats. Her debut collection of poetry, *Thursdays with You*, was released in September 2023 and reflects her unique voice and emotional depth. Through her evocative verses, Emma captures the beauty and complexity of relationships, inviting readers to experience moments of vulnerability and joy. As she continues to write, Emma aims to foster a deeper understanding of human experience, drawing from her life and the world around her. With a keen eye for detail and a heartfelt approach, she is excited to share her journey as a poet and to connect with others through her words.